BUG BOOKS

Cockroach

Karen Hartley, Chris Macro, and Philip Taylor

Heinemann Library
Chicago, Illinois

Customer Service 888-454-2279
Visit our website at www.heinemannraintree.com

Designed by Ron Kamen, Michelle Lisseter, and Bridge Creative Services Limited
Illustrations by Alan Fraser at Pennant Illustration
Printed in China by South China Printing Company

10 09 08 07 06
10 9 8 7 6 5 4 3 2 1

New edition ISBN: 1-4034-8296-9 (hardcover)
              1-4034-8309-4 (paperback)

The Library of Congress has cataloged the first edition as follows:
Hartley, Karen, 1949-
        Cockroach / Karen Hartley, Chris Macro, and Philip Taylor.
            p. cm. -- (Bug books)
        Includes bibliographical references and index.
        Summary: A simple introduction to the physical characteristics, diet, life cycle, predators,
                    habitat, and lifespan of cockroaches.
        ISBN 1-57572-797-8 (lib. bdg.)
        1. Cockroaches—Juvenile literature. [1. Cockroaches.] I. Macro, Chris, 1940-. II. Taylor,
        Philip, 1949-. III. Title. IV. Series.
        QL505.5.H28   1999
        595.7'28—dc21   98-42678
                            CIP
                            AC

Acknowledgments
The author and publishers are grateful to the following for permission to reproduce photographs:
Ardea: P Goetgheluck pp. 6, 10, 22, J Mason pp. 14, 24, 27, A Weaving pp. 12, 26; Bruce
Coleman Ltd: A Purcell p. 21, K Taylor pp. 11, 19, 23, 25, 28, C Varndell p. 16, R Williams p. 5;
Trevor Clifford: p. 29; NHPA: ANT p. 9, B Love p. 13, G Bernard p. 17, S Dalton pp. 4 15,
M Garwood p. 20, D Heuclin p. 18; Okapia: M Kage p. 7, N Lange p. 8.

Cover photograph reproduced with permission of NHPA/Image Quest 3-D.

The publishers would like to thank Nancy Harris for her assistance in the preparation of this book.

Every effort has been made to contact copyright holders of any material reproduced in this
book. Any omissions will be rectified in subsequent printings if notice is given to the publisher.

The paper used to print this book comes from sustainable sources.

Some words are shown in bold, **like this**. You can find out what they mean
by looking in the glossary.

Contents

What Are Cockroaches?

Cockroaches are **insects**. They are **pests** because they carry harmful **germs**. Germs can make people sick.

4

There are many different types of cockroaches. They live all over the world.

Cockroaches have flat bodies.
They have six long,
hairy legs.

legs

feeler

Cockroaches have two pairs of wings.
They have a pair of long **feelers** on
their heads. They have small claws on
their feet.

Some cockroaches are big and
some are small. In colder countries,
cockroaches are very small. Some of
them can fit on a small button or coin.

8

Cockroaches that live in hot countries can be much bigger. They can be as long as an adult's finger.

ant

cockroach

How Are Cockroaches Born?

Some **female** cockroaches lay their eggs in cases, called **purses**. The purses protect the eggs and stop them from drying out.

purse

Some cockroaches carry their eggs
in the purses until they are ready to
hatch. This can take eight weeks.

How Do Cockroaches Grow?

Young cockroaches are called **nymphs**. They do not have wings. As they grow they get too big for their skin. The skin splits and the nymph crawls out.

nymph

nymph

old skin

A new skin has grown under the old one. This is called **molting**. Cockroaches molt six or eight times before they are fully grown.

What Do Cockroaches Eat?

Cockroaches usually eat dead plants or animals, such as this centipede.

14

Cockroaches eat almost anything. They will even eat the glue from the back of postage stamps.

Which Animals Eat Cockroaches?

Lizards, frogs, and birds like to eat cockroaches if they can catch them.

16

Other **insects**, such as ants, sometimes eat cockroaches. Some cockroaches can tuck their legs in and lie very flat to protect themselves.

17

How Do Cockroaches Move?

Cockroaches have long legs and can run very fast. They usually move with their heads down because they are looking on the ground for food.

Even though they have two pairs of wings, only some cockroaches can fly. The **females** have smaller wings. Very few females can fly.

Where Do Cockroaches Live?

Most cockroaches like to live in warm places. They cannot live in cold places. In some countries many live in warm buildings. Some live outdoors in the grass and in bushes.

20

Cockroaches often live in bakeries, kitchens, and restaurants where they can find scraps of food.

How Long Do Cockroaches Live?

Some cockroaches live for a few months. Others can live for two or three years.

Cockroaches live longer when the weather is cool, but not when it is too cold.

What Do Cockroaches Do?

Most cockroaches are **nocturnal**. This means they come out at night. Some cockroaches run away from bright lights.

Cockroaches are called **pests** because they crawl over our food and leave dirt and **germs** on it. If we ate the food it would probably make us sick.

How Are Cockroaches Special?

Cockroaches are very important to other plants and animals because they make the soil better. They break up dead leaves and animal droppings.

Cockroaches have two special little **feelers** at the back end of their bodies. These can feel the air moving when other animals are close. This tells the cockroaches when they are in danger.

back feeler

Thinking About Cockroaches

This mother cockroach is carrying a special **purse**. Can you remember why she carries the purse with her?

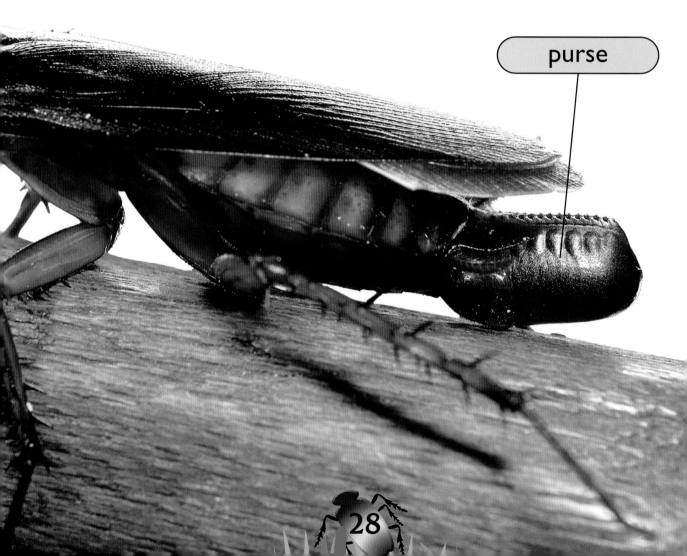

purse

We use fans to move air to keep us cool when it is hot. What does moving air tell the cockroach about other animals?

Bug Map

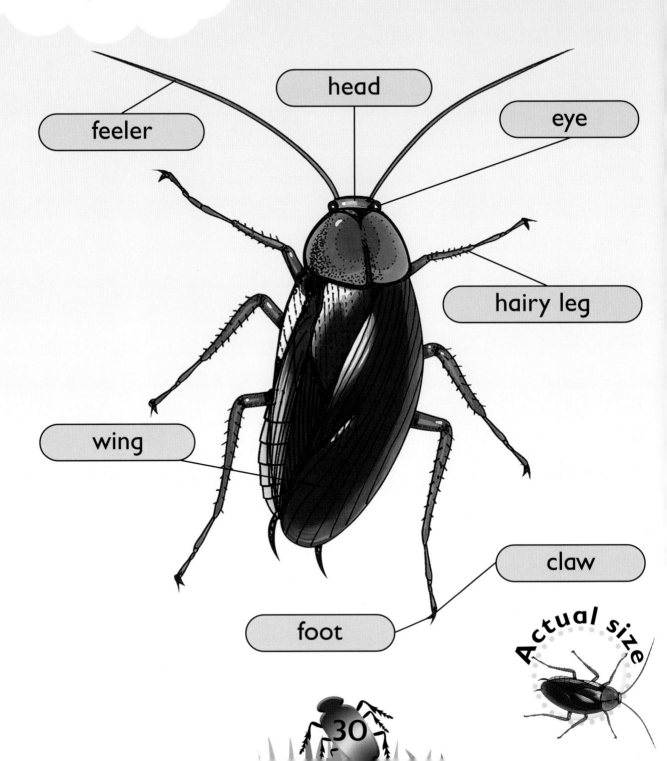

feeler

head

eye

hairy leg

wing

claw

foot

Actual size

Glossary

feelers thin growths from the head of an insect that help the insect to know what is around it

female girl

germs tiny creatures that cause diseases

hatch to come out of an egg

insect small animal with six legs

molt when a baby animal grows too big for its skin, it grows a new one. The old one falls off.

nocturnal animal that sleeps in the day and comes out at night

nymph baby cockroach

pests animals that are a nuisance to people

purse special case that protects cockroach eggs

Index

More Books to Read

Dickmann, Nancy. *Cockroaches*.
  Chicago: Raintree, 2006.

Pyers, Greg. *Cockroaches Up Close*.
  Chicago: Raintree, 2005.